*Wry, wise, and whimsical, Barbara McLennan's aptly titled little book Surprised by Old Age is an eclectic potpourri of sage reflections, powerful quotes, whimsical verse, and poignant stories, her own and others. All of these, arranged around the haunting dilemma but possible delight of aging, do exactly what she intended them to do—touch us in "deep and sensitive places in the spirit." As a member of the group she addresses, I was moved and reminded that the last decades of life are in God's hands. They matter; they can be lived fully.*

--Dr. Rosalie de Rosset, Professor of Communications and Literature, Moody Bible Institute, Chicago

*What a wonderful book! It is a treasure of poetry, quotes, spiritual passages and stories. With each new bucket, a new set of emotions surface! It is heartfelt, vulnerable and authentic. Thank you, Barb, for evoking this experience.*

Patricia Moten Marshall, President of SynerChange Chicago

*Aging graciously, acting wisely, and serving responsibly are among life's vital tasks. Thankfully the how is not a secret. But who knew that a series of buckets could point the way! Captured in Barb McLennan's poetic images, used by others as vehicles for poignant reflection, sometimes serious, sometimes funny, many kinds of buckets illustrate important principles to keep a healthy "surprise" in old age.*

--Linda Cannell, former academic dean at North Park Theological Seminary, Former professor at Gordon-Conwell Theological Seminary and Trinity Evangelical Divinity School in Chicago.

*Barbara McLennan has charmed countless people over the years with her creative writing and artwork.  In Surprised by Old Age, Barbara opens her heart and life to us with her unique blend of humor, delight, angst, confusion, fear, and anticipation that is felt and readily absorbed by all of us.  The reader will be warmly welcomed by Barbara to laugh a lot, cry a little, and confidently celebrate with joy what can yet be a glorious future.*

--Rev. Douglas Barram, pastor, Young Life leader, community developer

*As her pastor, ministry teammate, and friend, I've witnessed Barb McLennan build a godly legacy. She shares her unique blend of wisdom and wit in Surprised by Old Age. She introduces us to a diverse cast of characters who provide concrete examples of what it means to "number our days that we may gain a heart of wisdom" (Psalm 90:12).*

Eric Flood, senior pastor at South Park Church

May 21, 2022

To Kim —
A special person in a very
special family.
Fondly,
Barbara McLennan

# Surprised by Old Age
## From A Bucket List to a List of Buckets

# Surprised by Old Age

## From a Bucket List to a List of Buckets

*Blessings,*
*Barbara McLennan*

## By Barbara McLennan

*Surprised by Old Age*

Copyright © 2018 by Barbara McLennan

Cover design by Todd McLennan
www.toddmclennanphotography.com

Published in cooperation with A Powerful Story
www.APowerfulStory.com

Published by A Powerful Story
Printed in United States of American

ISBN-13: 978-0-9909222-7-8

## Dedication

*To my prime encourager, Jim—my husband of sixty years.*
*To our four children, and spouses and*
*all nine of our grandchildren…*
*each of whom have loved me well*
*and have kept me young at heart*
*regardless of age.*

*I also dedicate this book to the memory of my mom,*
*Hanna Schultz, who lived into her hundredth year.*
*She was my model and hero for aging with grace.*

# Contents

# Preface

## How Did We Get Here?

"Old Age."

Two common words I've been hearing of late,
    As I chatter with friends and begin to relate
    Those "organ recitals" of our aches and pains—
    Life's season about which we like to complain.

We tell of "fake joints" all shiny and new
    (Made of titanium), and our surgeries too.
    Hearing aids, implants, toupees and more,
    Sleep aids and Medicare come to the fore.

How did we get here? It happened so fast—
    Less time is ahead, while much more has passed.
    Old Age just sneaks up without warning or clue,
    Surprising its victims—universally true!

"Certainly not me" and "surely not yet"—
 "That's just for others," I'm willing to bet.
 "I feel like I'm forty, or perhaps sixty-two,
 But I'm almost eighty—Can that really be true?"

"You're only as old as you feel," so they say.
 Well, I'm havin' fun and still makin' hay.
 My words may say one thing yet my "bod"
 another—
 'Cause it takes a lot longer when I need to recover.

Old Age's arrival holds shades of denial
 Like memory failures becoming a trial,
 Plus changes in shape and wrinkles galore,
 Naps every day and way too much more.

Hair's getting sparse, now most of it's white,
 And I find it in places I'm sure are not right.
 Decades dash by, and they're picking up speed.
 "Please slow it down" is now what I plead.

That inevitable season has come without doubt,
 Yet my goals are consistent with what I'm about.
 My soul's deepest yearning—to finish well—
 whatever that means my next years will tell.

To grow old in God's grace, to spread lots of love,
 And continue in faith, which comes from above.

# Introduction

Life is full of surprises, which seem to multiply in
this season of Old Age! They arrive in the form of
unanticipated, unexpected, and sometimes unwelcomed
issues and events. Perhaps the most perplexing surprise
of all, after seasons of observing those elderly types—
senior citizens, old folks, gentle walkers—was the
realization that I had become one of them!

In my college years, I considered thirty to be "old." I
blinked once, and it was I blowing out thirty candles on
my cake! At that age, I was certain age fifty would surely
be old. Then I blinked again, and I was fifty! But I still
didn't feel old at all!

It was not until our eldest daughter turned fifty that my
advancing age really began to sink in. It was clear that
my perception of Old Age with all of its realities had
continued to become more and more elastic through the
seasons of life. Recently, aging issues have descended
on me with increasing speed and intensity. I now find

many others in my circle of friends and acquaintances that relate to my experiences—definitely surprising and often shocking to all of us! Alongside changes in physical appearance, mental "brain burps" and medical interruptions, came the nagging, niggling wish to "finish well" in the coming chapter of my life. But how?

With my milestone 80th birthday fast approaching (or more accurately, breathing hotly down my neck), I toyed with the idea of writing a book about old age. In search of a catchy title, I hoped for a melodious euphemism like *Legacy Milestones, Tarnish on the Golden Years, The Chill of Winter, Youthfully Challenged,* or even just plain *Aging.* No matter how I tried to wrap it up, it still amounted to the same thing. Lots more candles on my cake! *Surprised by Old Age* emerged as the clear winner!

Surprise is the recurring theme in conversations about aging. When I talk with my contemporaries, we all seem to be asking the same questions: "How did I get here? How did I miss all the clues leading up to this season? Who is that imposter who keeps sneaking between me and my mirror?" I confess, it did take me by surprise.

The aging process can take many different paths. A person can passively accept it, sit in a rocker and become invisible. We can grit our teeth (if we still have them) and resist, or we can fight getting old with everything that's in us! Another option might be to milk it and capitalize on it as a place of honor and entitlement. Or we can just playfully seek to laugh it off and have some fun! I suspect in the end, it amounts to a little of each of these. Bottom line, my goal is to "finish well"!

Literature and film are replete with themes of aging— some hilarious, some pathetic, a few helpful and most painfully true—and all are a little too close to reality to ignore.

I began pondering a crucial question: "What would be a possible metaphor to inform my journey into aging?" As I wrestled with this, I stumbled upon the 2007 movie, *The Bucket List,* starring Morgan Freeman and Jack Nicholson. This award-winning film influenced the perception of old age in our culture and introduced the term "bucket list" into the vernacular until it became a common, everyday American practice. Don't you have a "bucket list"?

Buckets serve as a widely-used metaphor, from phrases like "a drop in the bucket" to the indelicate idiom "kicking the bucket." I began to think not only about a bucket list, but also a list of buckets!

Being an incurable poet, I began writing poems, which tied together Old Age with the various and sundry buckets of life. As my collection of poems grew, the skeleton of this book, *Surprised by Old Age: From a Bucket List to a List of Buckets,* began to take shape. Casual conversation with my contemporaries, revealing only this title, elicited their stories, which would potentially become meat on the poetic bones.

As I have gathered stories and created poems to relate my impressions of this season of life, I appreciate the many friends and family who have contributed story ideas. I hope to shed a little whimsy and insight to help you navigate the Golden Years and finish well.

# Chapter One

## A Drop in the Bucket

A drop in the bucket took a moment in time
    When everything changed—it was all on the line.
    Things started out harmless, or so it did seem
    Like that wee, little drop, or the wisp of a dream.

Perhaps just a whim, or a new road to try
    Which led to another, and soon by and by,
    A habit was formed, then a life-changing trend—
    A pattern established—who knew to what end.

More drops in my bucket sounded simple enough,
    Yet they shaped and they formed my very core stuff.
    The drops became puddles, soon filled me half way;
    My bucket was altered by work and by play.

Approaching life's end I wonder just how
    I got to this place where I find myself now.

Those drops in my bucket have filled and defined
Both body and soul, not to mention my mind.

Even now in this season, which we call "Old Age,"
A new drop can still impact my life's final page.
Be it joyous or grievous, it is just a part
Of what God chooses to give me from His loving
heart.

He guides my direction, be it easy or rough.
He'll decide when my bucket is quite full enough.
So I take every drop as from His strong hand,
To embrace with joy, every day that I can.

# Roger The American

*Tuesday, 6 June 1944. D-Day. "The Day of Infamy." Compared to all that happened that day on Normandy's Omaha Beach, this story amounts to a drop in the bucket—a miniscule drop at that. But it is still astonishing. Roger is a friend of my brother-in-law Bill, who told us this story as we traveled the Normandy shore. Being there made the story even more poignant.*

Roger had fought at Normandy. He revisited the infamous beach 50 years later, during the half-century celebration of the WWII landing of 156,000 Allied troops which turned the tide of the war.

Roger brought his wife and son back to the place where he scaled the steep cliff that stormy June day. Huge craters provided lingering evidence of the bombings that riddled the countryside in that battle. Three thousand of Roger's comrades lay wounded and many more dead behind him as he sprinted to the top of that beachside hill. Five decades later, only a few German bunkers were now still visible. These housed deadly Nazi machine gun nests and now were grown over with lush green grass. Roger's family stood in awe.

"This is the exact spot where I stood after scaling the cliff." Roger stated with confidence.

His wife tilted her head to the side. "How can you know exactly?"

"See that church out in the distance? Now look at this cottage and old barn here to our right. Those two landmarks lined up just as they do now. I'm sure this is the place."

Just then, an old French woman rushed up to them, tugged at Roger's sleeve and broke into their conversation, "Monsieur, do you speak French?"

"Why yes, yes I do."

"Are you American? Is your name Roger?"

Completely taken aback, Roger stammered, "Yes, I am American, and yes, I am Roger!"

"Follow me." She turned and led them to the cottage.

The woman opened the door and motioned for them to follow. Once inside, she reached into a corner cabinet and pulled out an old bottle of wine, thick with dust. She quickly wiped it off, revealing a label, which read "For Roger, the American." She proudly handed it to Roger and then slowly backed away. Head bowed slightly, the French woman whispered in broken English, "I knew you would come back someday. You saved my life."

"I don't remember saving any woman's life that day. What on earth are you talking about?"

The woman motioned for them to sit at her modest table, and she began telling her story. "In all the confusion that day, I heard one American soldier speaking French. I pled with you to move the Jeep your officer had parked near my barn. I owned one cow—the only way I was able to eat and stay alive. I knew the Nazis would eventually see the Jeep from the air and drop bombs. Because you moved your Jeep, I was able to survive. Thank you, thank you for saving my life!"

"But how did you find me after all these years?"

"The men, the soldiers, many come back year after year. On every anniversary, I wander around, listening and looking. I knew I would never forget your kind face, and I recognized your voice somehow. Something told me you would be here this time—on the 50th anniversary. I'm so happy to thank you for saving my life!"

Just a drop in the bucket for Roger. Life and death for her.

# Rare Air

My husband, Jim, and I sat in the front row as we
listened to remarks from an FAA representative presiding
over the award ceremony. It became clear that Jim was
entering "rare air" so to speak, as we heard of previous
notable recipients like astronaut Chuck Yeager and
famed stunt pilot Bob Hoover. Being awarded the Wright
Brothers "Master Pilot" Award for 50 years of incident-
free flying affirmed Jim's lifelong passion for aviation.
His flying career has actually spanned 60 plus years and
is still going strong. But his aviation beginnings dated
back to 1944, when he was just a formative young lad.
His two uncles were bomber pilots in WWII, and he
remembers praying nightly for their safe return. They
both came home as decorated heroes.

Jim spoke fondly of his uncles. "After the war Uncle Lyle
settled in a nearby town and became the Sunday school
teacher for my class of ten-year-old boys. He challenged
us to memorize Bible verses and rewarded our efforts
with the promise of an airplane ride in exchange for
memorizing one hundred verses. I was captured hook,
line and sinker, and I feverishly labored over the prospect
of that airplane ride. Sure enough, after months of
effort, I reached verse one hundred. I was over-the-top
elated when I climbed into that small Navion airplane. I
remember fantasizing that I owned it. As I disembarked,
I vowed that someday I would learn to fly and own

my own airplane. From that day on, my dreams and drawings were of airplanes with me as the pilot."

That experience, one small drop in the bucket of Jim's life, turned out to be more than just a passing fancy. His fascination with flight and aviation continued.

In 1954, his freshman year at Wheaton College, Jim learned of a college flying club run by a chemistry professor who owned a Luscombe plane. For the grand cost of $4 an hour (including gas) to rent the plane, plus just $4 for the instructor, Jim found himself in the cockpit. That first flight instructor was an out-of-the-ordinary, gung-ho, ex-military guy. Jim's very first lesson was spent doing spins, instead of the usual rudimentary basics. His instructor harshly informed him, "if you can't recover from a spin, you don't belong in the air." That day he learned about spins even before he learned to land the airplane.

Jim's Pilot Log Book currently shows over two thousand hours of flying time. Even at age 82, he still flies his own airplane, a Citation Mustang Jet. Jim uses it frequently, as he says, "Not only for the thrill of flying and sense of accomplishment, but for the joy of building and servicing important relationships with friends and family nationwide. The country has shrunk in size, giving us coast-to-coast options to be with people, otherwise not possible. A bonus has been the opportunity to make new friends in the brotherhood of aviators."

What may have seemed simply a creative way to get a young boy to memorize Scripture, a small drop in the bucket of his life, turned out to be significant in many ways.

*Barbara McLennan*

**There is always one moment in childhood**

**When the door opens and lets the future in.**[1]


—Graham Greene

---

1    Graham Greene, The Power and the Glory (New York, Penquin Classics, 2003). Originally published 1940.

# A Drop That Started a New Career

My working definition of a "drop in the bucket" includes concepts of change and trajectory. One small event, a minor change in direction of only a few degrees, can impact our journey dramatically. Even as an inch of error in launching a rocket will result in miles of missing the target, a new or slightly altered life direction, though a minor "drop" now, will spread and grow to influence future outcomes in astounding ways. Whether a memorable "drop" comes early or late in life, it is important to name it and claim it. Change is not easy, but it is inevitable. Embrace it, and it might take you somewhere delightful.

My experience of becoming a published author unexpectedly started at age 75, when a drop in my bucket occurred at a 55th college reunion dinner. This turned out to be my best surprise of old age so far. I had often dreamed of publishing some of my writing, particularly poetry, though I never imagined it would happen. Yet two of my poems appear as the prologue and epilogue of a good friend's book. Not only did it include my poetry, but it also opened the door to collaborate with him in re-writing his whole book, *(in)visible: from obscure to valuable* [2].

A leap of faith carried me into this project, as I hardly knew this man. Dr. Arthur J. Ammann, a noted pediatric

---

2   *(in)visible...from obscure to valuable* by Arthur J Ammann with Barbara McLennan, Wipf and Stock Publishers, 2014

immunologist from San Francisco was a college friend of Jim's, but they'd been worlds apart for decades. Although I had been writing for myself since high school days, I had never tried to publish. This looked like my chance to fulfill that dream. The learning curve was steep but intriguing and challenging. It involved four-hour phone conversations. We had to work around a three-hour time difference, Florida to California. Another real challenge came in learning the art of collaboration. How did two people do this?

Early on, I asked Art, "Do you want me to be nice or honest?"

His answer, of course, "Honest."

So we combed through every sentence in his collection of stories that had been stashed away for the past 45 years.

As a physician who conducted groundbreaking scientific research, he had been catapulted into the HIV/AIDS epidemic from the very start in 1981. Being a compassionate champion of the disadvantaged, as well as an instinctive storyteller, his experiences came alive on every page. I was honored to enter into this project with him and experienced tremendous growth in the process.

Long after we came up with the title of "invisible, from obscure to valuable," we realized various aspects of our subject applied to us. First, the stories themselves had been all but invisible for many years—sitting on the shelf, unnoticed. Now, as Art dusted them off and attempted to breathe life into them, they grew in value. Also, we recognized that Art and I were virtually obscure and invisible to each other, not having met until the college reunion. We were living proof of the overall theme of our book, which emphasizes the fact that God brings individuals into our life for a reason. No matter how obscure or insignificant they may seem, the experience of interaction with them transforms both individuals. They discover mutual value—and in our case, created something of value by collaborating. The friendship we forged through this process was rich and transformative for me and provided a valued relationship for us as couples as well.

Now I'm eager to see what's next!

# Chapter Two

## The Bucket Brigade

When a school was on fire in the good old days,
    Or a house or barn was suddenly ablaze,
    The word was sent out with a clarion shout.
    Everyone knew what that call was about!
    "We need help quickly, get here post haste!
    Drop everything! There's no time to waste!"

Back then it was called the Bucket Brigade—
    As folks came from all over to form a "parade."
    At one end was water; the other end fire,
    Bucket by bucket, the flames did expire.

When crisis occurs with a life in distress,
    Friends, family and neighbors clean up the mess.
    They join in together to form a "brigade,"
    Their care and concern so clearly displayed.

We all will need help some time it's true
    That's when our brigade is sure to come through.

Now looking back with heartfelt scrutiny
    Life's at its best when lived in community.
    Blessing each other with kind word and deed,
    Bucket in hand whenever a need.

# Bucket Parade

Thinking of my own Bucket Brigade, I realized that one of the crucial tools of keeping valued relationships alive over the years has simply been the sending of Christmas cards. In recent years, I have managed to simplify a bit—reducing my inordinate amount of décor, gift-buying and general frenzy associated with Christmases' past. But I have not been able to shake my tradition of creating our elaborate family Christmas pictorial greeting.

Please understand, this practice had evolved gradually over six decades of married life. It started out simply with a single letter-sized sheet of paper, black on white, with one family portrait and a few candid photos. Quite honestly, it was also a way of saving funds on our tight Christmas budget early in marriage. A photocopied letter was cheaper than fancy Christmas cards. Along with the growth of our family came the growth of the greeting, with dozens of photos and several poems—all on a double sheet of paper, printed in color, both sides of the page. If a picture is worth a thousand words, do the math! It had become a major production.

I love sending this annual newsletter. However as November approaches each year, I am struck with panic—overcome by the reality that Christmas is right around the corner, and time has come to start my creative process.

So, what about my "parade"? As the actual Christmas greeting expanded in size, so did the mailing list. Starting with about a hundred names, it has increased to an almost unmanageable five hundred addresses. With some, our only remaining contact is the exchange of Christmas cards. It is amazing to me how this annual tool serves to maintain a sense of closeness within precious relationships otherwise lost. As I fasten each printed label to an oversized envelope, I think of that person and our history, having shared some season of life together—be it brief or lengthy. From A to Z, Adams to Zimmanck, they seem to form a parade. They have marched through my life—paths crossing for a time, then wandering off as the parade continues through the years. Names drop off, new ones appear; yet most remain through thick and thin.

As I stand at the curb, cheering my parade, waving my flag of greeting, I notice a curious phenomenon: *they each are holding a bucket!* I am ever grateful for each individual who has helped extinguish my crisis fires at critical times of my life. I continue to be blessed by the rich relationships that remain. They are my community, across the nation, even across the globe. This is one Christmas tradition I won't be quick to eliminate.

*Barbara McLennan*

*I wrote this poem on the eve of my husband Jim's 80th birthday. I frequently include a copy in birthday cards to friends turning 80. Each time, I'm reminded of what a blessing it is to have friends whom I've known for decades. Studies show that our physical and mental health is influenced most by our social connections. I'm thankful for my "bucket brigade" and that I can celebrate the 80th birthdays of so many friends!*

# Making Music at Eighty

A musical octave has eight lines and spaces.
    Notes placed upon them form tunes from their places.
    The clefs—bass or treble—make songs high or low.
    Two numbers count rhythm—the beat fast or slow.
    Harmonies and scales take the piece up and down;
    The melody and mood produce pleasing sound.

An octave of decades marks eighty years old,
    So we celebrate the story, which this life has told.
    Many measures have passed throughout the years—
    Many were happy, though some did hold tears.

Born in a day so dark with war—
    Depression as well—with hardships galore.
    Life's heavy dirges created a mess,
    But light, springy melodies soon brought happiness.

Loudly or softly—tunes fast or slow,
    Eighty years making music—a wonderful show.

There were strong refrains, with recurring reprises
    Then slowing a bit like soft summer breezes.
    The symphony is not yet complete,
    Now with more rests and stops—but still that great
    beat.

We celebrate eighty and sing right along,
    Honored and happy to be part of your song.

*Barbara McLennan*

**The legacy you leave is what lives on**

**in the people you love.**

—From a sermon entitled
"What does it mean to finish well?"

by Rev. Dr. Eric Flood,
South Park Church, Park Ridge, IL

# Chapter Three

*This chapter was inspired by a children's camp song made popular in 1960 by folk singers Harry Belafonte and Odetta. The true origins date back to Germany in the mid 1800s. As with many camp songs the lyrics keep on repeating, ending right back where it started.*

## A Hole in the Bucket

There's a hole in your bucket, dear Liza and Henry.
> There's a hole in your bucket, dear Liza, a hole.
> There's a lot of stuff needed, dear Liza and Henry,
> Stuff you don't have if fixing's your goal.
> Some straw would fill it, but straw is too long—
> And an axe would sure cut it, we learn in the song.
> But the axe is too dull, and you'll need a stone
> To sharpen the blade you will sure need to hone.
> But that stone needs some water so it's back to the start,
> 'Cuz the bucket's all leaky and falling apart.

So there you have it—a story of life,
>Told by dear Henry and Liza, his wife.
>What an impasse those dear folks were in—
>A circular battle they just couldn't win.

Now as I ponder the subject of holes,
>I can't help but see that they're taking their tolls.
>There's a hole in my memory, where things just
>leak out—
>So let's blame it on age—I have little doubt.

There's a pain in my back and one in my knee—
>A hole called arthritis, but there's more, can't
>you see?
>There's a hole in my heart left by loved ones
>who've died,
>Goodness knows the buckets of tears I have cried.

Our nation is broken—so newscasters say—
>We see the sad evidence day after day.
>The news is so grim that I don't want to hear it;
>There's a hole in our country, and many do fear it.
>It all seems as hopeless as the old Bucket Song,
>But wait, there's Good News, amazing and strong.

God created us all—each one with a soul,
>With a space for Himself—you might call it a hole,

*Barbara McLennan*

Whose shape and size are filled only by Him,
Which He offers to all who would let Him come in.

That big hole will be filled, and thus ends our story—
With Him forever—to God be the glory!

# Holes Where My Tears Leaked Out

Early in 2016, I was diagnosed with cancer, and so was my well-loved son-in-law, Bill Ostlund (we always called him Ozzie). I survived with successful surgery and no ongoing treatment. I felt grateful and blessed.

But Ozzie did not survive. His surgery was routine and successful, but the chemo treatments took his life. By May of 2016, he was gone. Ozzie was in his late 50s, as is my daughter, Tami, now his widow.

Never has our whole family experienced such deep grief! For me, it has been like trying to climb out of a deep pit. I would think I was just about out, then my foothold seemed to give way and I would slip backward into the abyss.

Thankfully, God was always there to catch me and hold me tight. He did not immediately lift me out of the pit, but He remained there, always by my side, with comfort and strength, assuring me that this is a long process and this too shall pass. But that process is surprisingly hard.

Two months after Ozzie's death, I sat on my patio, experiencing the first cool, refreshing day after an oppressively hot, stormy July. I pondered the forming and writing of this book. The project had started out light and airy, with whimsical rhymes—a chance to laugh at my dilemma of aging. But as time passed, and I began to write, the book began touching deep, sensitive places. That particular morning I asked myself the very opening question of the book, "How did I get here?" Not questioning my age, but my state of mind. How did I get here, to this particular morning, piecing together intense sadness, fear and a sense of helplessness? My writing, often poetry, normally reflects my current state of mind and experience, but quite honestly, I never expected to be where I found myself that day, unable to write a single word. Indeed a surprise, and not a good one. For the first time, I realized that my ability to finish well hung in the balance of how I handled this experience of loss and grief. I found myself drowning in perilous waves of fear, engulfed in an ocean of tears.

I picked up a little devotional book, titled simply *Musings*, written by a dear friend, Kent Hotaling. Two of the quotes he'd collected arrested me:

"Tears remind us of our vulnerability, they call us to yield our desire to control things, and be with what is…. Tears are a sign of beginning to come undone, which means that the divine has room to enter."[3]

And then another; "The paradox of grief is that it is healing: it somehow restores our souls, when all

---

3    Christine Valters Paintner, *The Unraveling Toward Love*. Kent quoted her from an article in Weavings Journal, but the article can also be found at: https://abbeyofthearts.com/blog/2017/09/10/the-unraveling-toward-love-a-love-note-from-your-online-abbess/

the while we thought it would leave us in despair. Control is the enemy; grief is our friend."[4]

Right there, in the turmoil of heart and spirit, I faced my own mortality. I felt so grateful to survive, yet a myriad of questions still loomed. Why was Ozzie taken from us so young? Why did I survive and he did not? What happens to our faith when God does not answer our heartfelt prayers in the way that we want? In the quiet that so often follows a storm, a verse from Romans 8:38-39 came flooding back to mind and flowed over me like an elixir, "I am convinced that neither death nor life… nor things present nor to come…nor anything in all creation will be able to separate us from the love of God."

Just then an epiphany, which I had experienced years ago came flooding back to my heart and mind. It was a vivid, enhanced realization of God's love for me as His child. The words jumped out to me from the pages of my Bible—"You are my Beloved." Even in the midst of this great sorrow I could rest in my identity as "Beloved." My heart began to feel peace…that unique peace from God that "passes understanding."

Though I still feel that painful hole Ozzie's death left in my heart, and I'm still certain that the old are not meant to bury the young, I remain convinced and grateful that I'll see our beloved Ozzie again on the other side of this earthly life.

---

4    John Eldredge, The Journey of Desire (Nashville, Thomas Nelson Publishers, 2016)

**Keep it simple. Show up. Go to the hard places.**

**Be joyful and play. Love Jesus. Love people.**

— Bill "Ozzie" Ostlund

60 years young (April 28, 1957 - April 30, 2017)

# The Hole Left By Bill

*April 28, 1957 to April 30, 2017*

To Bill, the one and only Bill.
    His shoes are massive ones to fill,
    Let alone his skates or boots,
    Skiing the hill with hollers and hoots.

Sixty years young and so much fun—
    Life packed with sports—at least a ton.
    But there was more to Bill you see,
    His fierce love for family.

First for Tam, a match, you bet,
    Then Ellen and Mark, the best kids yet—
    And Brendan and Abby complete the set.
    But then came Davis and little Linc,
    Bill's greatest joys, don't you think?

Free Spirit describes a life full of thrills,
    With compassion for others—his people skills.
    To us he was another true son
    With his love and warmth, just full of fun.

Jesus was IN him as he walked this earth
    Living life to the fullest for all he was worth.
    Now he's WITH Jesus, Bill's best friend.
    He's with Him in Heaven, singing praise without
    end.

**You cannot walk the second journey with the first journey tools.**

**You need a whole new tool set.**[5]

—Richard Rohr

---

5    Richard Rohr, *Falling Upward: A Spirituality for the Two Halves of Life* (San Francisco, Jossey-Bass, 2011)

# Psalm 23, NIV

¹ The Lord is my shepherd, I lack nothing.
² He makes me lie down in green pastures,
he leads me beside quiet waters,
³ he refreshes my soul.
He guides me along the right paths
for his name's sake.
⁴ Even though I walk
through the darkest valley,
I will fear no evil,
for you are with me;
your rod and your staff,
they comfort me.

⁵ You prepare a table before me
in the presence of my enemies.
You anoint my head with oil;
my cup overflows.
⁶ Surely your goodness and love will follow me
all the days of my life,
and I will dwell in the house of the Lord
forever.

*Barbara McLennan*

# Shepherd and Host

*Rev. Dr. William G Enright is a very close college friend, and retired Senior Pastor of Second Presbyterian Church Indianapolis. He kindly offered this reflection on Psalm 23 (see previous pag)e. When we find ourselves holding a bucket of tears, or a bucket with holes, we can easily give in to fear. But in those moments, Dr. Enright reminds us, we need not fear. Not because of our own courage, but because God is a good shepherd, and He is with us in every circumstance.*

In my daily study, I'm rereading (and rethinking) the Psalms. So, today was Psalm 23. This psalm focuses on the character of the Lord as shepherd (v. 1-4) and as the ultimate host (v. 5-6).

The psalm is also a personal confession of faith and trust that makes all the difference as to how I see and experience life. I am the one who has been blessed; I need not give in to my fears.

"Fear not" is the good news that permits me to live through failure, disappointment, illness, even the specter of death itself. I am not alone as the Shepherd is with me and never do I walk alone.

# Holes and Tunnels

Holes don't just happen.
　　They are the result of many strokes—
　　Deliberate, determined picking and shoveling.
　　Or they are the product of erosion—
　　Relentless wearing away by time and elements.
　　Tunnels, likewise, are so created,
　　Often with purpose and direction,
　　Yet sometimes abandoned for a better way.
　　At certain moments in my life,
　　I feel that I am in foxhole—
　　Useful for a while
　　Now, I'm trying to get out—

Or I'm in a dark tunnel searching for light.
　　The hole didn't just happen.
　　Nor did that dark tunnel.
　　I dug it unwittingly or knowingly,
　　or I stupidly fell into some existing cavern.
　　Perhaps I wandered into a fascinating crevice
　　Which turned out to be a burdensome tunnel,
　　Too complicated, too lengthy to maneuver,
　　And I'm too scared, too tired to turn back.
　　O God, are you Lord of holes and tunnels?
　　Do you care about my misery and frustration?

Do you forgive my digging, my falling in, my
wandering, which brought me to this awful place?

What relief! What joy! What undeserving favor!
　　You scoop me up and light the way.
　　You alone provide the way out,
　　My God and my Savior!!
　　And what is more—

You still don't take away my shovel!

(Barbara McLennan, 1982)

# Passing the Bucket? Or Owning the Bucket?

*Midge was my high school pal; we attended the same church and the same college. We shared a place in our high school "Senior Superlatives," voted "Best Writers" in our class of over 500. After her wedding I lost touch with her, but 50 years later at our college reunion, we reconnected and re-bonded. There she courageously related her painful life story before our entire class gathering. It was compelling, raw and jarring compared to most.*

*In response to my request, Midge shared her journey. She admitted that her first response to betrayal was seeing herself as a victim, blaming others and feeling abandoned. But ultimately, she traded her bucket of pain for one overflowing with love. No longer a victim, she owned her identity as a deeply loved child of God. Here is what she wrote:*

Betrayal is gut wrenching. Having factual proof of it is devastating, but living in the shadows of denial as to its truth emboldens a peculiar cruelty. Being stonewalled in knowing the truth while living in the murky gray fog of an ongoing cover up, one that suggested a normal marriage and family, created an emotional and mental stigmatism that had my life in a sense of perpetual free fall.

The garage door would go up and down, and there would be long periods of absence. Subtle distancing behaviors that denied eye contact, the use of my name or the sharing of intimacy became the norm at home, while in a public setting we looked like best friends. Keeping a happy, positive face before the Christian college community of which we were a part proved taxing, but the greater torment was facing the reality of the abuse that was beginning to affect my mental, emotional and physical health.

Knowing about all the possibilities of my journey was impossible for me in the past, because I struggled way too much with the status of my ticket. Wanting to be a first-class Gucci traveler narrowed my options. Although the glasses looked smashing and effect was compelling, the meaning of the journey was a yawning chasm of either self-absorbed ventures or untouched possibilities. What people thought of me was powerful and created a performance mindset that fought against fear and failure at every turn.

When things fell apart, I tried to prop them up, to hide the truth. Eventually, I could no longer keep up appearances.

It was time to fully breathe. However, I saw admitting the truth about my life as a giveaway of everything I treasured—my family, our business, our finances, our friends and our future. The Christian community isn't known for being kind to those who screw up. The demise of my marriage and the sham it had become definitely qualified.

Secrets can be deadly as they often cover things that are intentionally kept in darkness when the light of truth is the precise revelation that brings life.

A bucket of secrets is a bucket of nothing!

I was living in a beautiful home on the hill with views of mountains and waters…sailboats and sunsets…but no one was home. The deafening quiet echoed the voices of family, friends and students who once filled this space. Disappointment, sorrow, grief and loss are cruel but honest companions when the composition and structure of relationships crumble. What was thought to be secure and safe has failed to live up to its billing. There must be someone to blame…someone to whom I can pass this bucket.

My view from a prostrate position on the closet floor was anything but expansive. No panorama, nothing majestic, no roar of the crowd there. Just the comfort of trampled carpet and pairs of shoes going nowhere. The cold reality of the moment hung in the air like an open window on a December morning. How did I end up with this bucket? What's in my bucket? Would anyone want to share my bucket? Not really. My bucket was empty.

Grief brings with it the potential cleansing of all kinds of debris. Like a power washer against a moss-covered wall, grief loosens the fragments of blame, judgment, comparison, self-justification, unfairness and that old standby un-forgiveness. And what to do with them?

Put them in my bucket! A much easier and less painful endeavor than choosing to face the fear from which I kept running to avoid having these hateful globs of truth actually strike me and lodge somewhere in my soul to create more intense pain. And what was I actually running from? Shame—the big lie that says I'm not good enough. The Accuser who night and day works the program, bullying me into the believing that I am not worth much of anything to anyone who really matters to me. Because if I were of value, I wouldn't have been lied to and abandoned!

However, there came the day—it was a Sunday in January—when I was totally spent in my loss and despair. I knew it was time to stop and drop. And there I was, face down amid my shoes and scarves wondering if there was a next step in the journey that would allow me to breathe normally and see the possibility of a new day, to say nothing of experiencing feelings that were peaceful and hopeful.

And this is what I heard my amazing Creator Father God say quietly in my heart: *You thought I wrote the story of Job to illustrate patience? I didn't. I want my children to know something else. I want you to know that just as I pointed out Job to Satan when he came to visit me in the heavenlies, I point out to him millions and millions of my children every day and say…'**This child will trust me in the darkness and will honor me as faithful.**'*

Taking ownership of my life, a visceral choice of my soul, was to agree with God about His thoughts concerning me when He designed and placed me on this earth. He's a Big Picture God of artistry, intellect and passion who made plans that I would utilize His design in ways that would make Him famous.

Learning to trust is hard. Learning to jump into my daddy's waiting arms in the swimming pool took some time and a big breath, but looking into the face of one I could trust, I jumped!

Seeing Jesus in the darkness of my closet and letting His love pour over my sore and aching soul began a process of trusting in the One who would never fail me, never leave me or ever forsake me.

And my bucket. Whatever happened to my bucket?

First, it was full of emptiness. Then it became full of resentment and hurt and pain and un-forgiveness, and then, very slowly, those contents began to dribble out— one forgiveness at a time, one gratitude at a time, one step of faith at a time.

Last time I checked, there still weren't any Gucci glasses, shoes or bags in my bucket. And that slight from a family member that I was hauling around, I decided to dump it out, too. My bucket is now filling up with grace and kindness and peace and favor that come from the Spirit of Jesus, and I carry it carefully and gratefully each day knowing that my steps are going somewhere good.

Somewhere good? Calling the steps of aging something positive can be a shock to the system. It certainly doesn't line up with voice of the culture. That voice talks about limitations, disabilities and, during the evening TV shows, advertises 43 different medications to eliminate the vicissitudes of aging—bad heart, diseased liver, weakened bladder and fragile bones.

And then there are those helpers and homes and lawyers and investments and insurance policies that can make one's incapacitation easier to bear, if one can afford them.

Experiencing the increasing helplessness and dependency that are part of the aging journey are not something to be looked forward to, are they? It is possible to protect my bucket from filling with the fears that come from not knowing, from being without, and from experiencing pain, loss and despair. Through my journey I am learning this amazing reality—that as I determine to rest in the truth of Jesus and choose to place my bucket in my Father's hands, stop trying to pass it, and cooperate with Him as to what goes into it—that I am loved, accepted, and set free.

# Chapter Four

## The Bucket List

Not too long ago, I started my list
    Of adventures and places I somehow have missed.
    My life has been full, but perhaps not enough,
    'Cause here still remains that additional stuff—

People to see, and places to go,
    More to explore—lots more to know.
    But wait! I suspect there is something amiss.
    This bucket means more than *doing* things missed.

It's much more than checking off stuff left undone—
    Like places to go for adventure and fun.
    'Cause relationships now are my priority—
    Not just things to *do*, but what's left to *be*.

Like forgiving, generosity, reconciling when needed—
    The real deal in this season is yet to be heeded.

Appropriate goals for life's farewell stage—
To enjoy peace, love and joy in this time called
Old Age.

In contrast, the Bucket List done in reverse—
Things ne'er to repeat, unkind acts and words terse,
Ideas I flubbed, adventures turned sour,
Stuff that drained energy as well as will power.

Forward or back, exciting or scary,
The Bucket List habit is still necessary.
We'll always need goals to keep looking ahead
To keep life moving forward without fear or dread.

# A Film Revisited

The first time I watched *The Bucket List,* a 2008 film starring Jack Nicholson and Morgan Freeman, I was approaching my 70th birthday. Ten years later, I revisited what had seemed to be an amusing comedy about doing the things you always wished you'd done. This time around, I found my perspective had shifted and my questions deepened. Was this a movie simply about shallow regret over things we have not accomplished or had opportunity to enjoy? Was it only about fulfilling my own wants and desires? Or was there more to a bucket list, like the need to include relationships with others?

Experiencing the movie again, as if for the first time, I was intrigued, and it touched me more deeply. Having had cancer myself as well as having lost our son-in-law to cancer within the past year, I saw the film in a new, much more personal way. A whole different meaning and rationale emerged.

The film pairs up two old dudes in a terminal cancer ward. The two men could not have been more different: one black, one white; one an ultra-rich executive, the other a blue-collar auto mechanic. Beyond those surface differences, it quickly becomes clear that these two men have very different approaches to life and ways of seeing the world. When they find themselves facing the shocking news that each has six months to live, more important differences are exposed—matters of the heart and mind. Their opposite lifelong attitudes and demeanor dictate the way in which they respond to their diminishing months of life.

The men conspire to escape the scene of hospital gowns and injections, trading them for audacious adventures to fulfill their newly invented "bucket lists." They successfully cross off experiences one by one, providing a series of entertaining moments. The list also becomes a tool to forge an unlikely, meaningful friendship between them. Their entire adventure brings about deep personal change in each of them as well.

As they compare lists and check off milestones, the men influence each other in transformational ways. For instance, Carter (Morgan Freeman) introduces the power of faith in God's goodness as they jet over the Polar Ice Cap viewing the overwhelming beauty of a staggering array of brilliant stars set in a black velvet night sky.

Unmoved, Edward (Jack Nicholson) denies any notion of faith or God. "I can't get my head around it."

Carter's terse and succinct reply? "Maybe your head gets in the way...what *do* you believe?"

Edward says, "I resist all beliefs."

Edward's wealth opens doors to magnificent travel experiences Carter could never have afforded: the pyramids, Himalayas and the Taj Mahal, to name a few. Laughter, fear, tears and temptation are woven into this season of unbridled adventure.

One day, Carter says, "Let's go home." He experiences a tearful reunion with his anxiously awaiting wife and family.

His grateful wife sobs and hugs him. "You left as a stranger and came back a husband."

Alas, all too soon, Carter's time runs out and he passes away—a contented and changed man. Edward's eulogy reveals his surprising change in spirit.

Edward, himself, has a bit more time, which he sorely needs in order to reconcile with his estranged daughter and meet his beautiful, little granddaughter for the first time. The clever, surprise-ending scene gives an appropriate finish to the whole film. The camera zooms in on the summit of Mt. Everest where two old coffee cans that hold the men's ashes are placed side by side. Turns out, the last item on their bucket list, though unfulfilled, was to summit Mt. Everest. Mission *accomplished.*

I saw the film differently at 80 because I felt more connected to the characters—both in age and circumstance. This time I was searching more for meaning than entertainment. I saw the core of the story to be about relationships, which color the nature of my bucket list. Instead of being inspired to write a bucket list, I was inspired to examine my relationships and to value them. I realized it was less about things to do, and more about things left to be.

**Old age is not a defeat but a victory,
not a punishment but a privilege.**

**One ought enter old age the way one enters
the senior year at a university,**

**in exciting anticipation of consummation.**[6]

—Rabbi Abraham Joshua Heschel

6    Abraham Joshua Heschel, *I Asked for Wonder: A Spiritual
      Anthology* (New York, The Crossroad Publishing Company,
      1983)

# Chapter Five

## A Bucket of Change

Nothing's as permanent as change, I've been told.
    For me, that goes double as I have grown old.
    Some changes are welcome, others not so.
    There's often no choice in the way things will go.

Our pace doesn't quicken; we can't jump as high.
    We don't sleep as well with more years rolling by.
    It happens to minds, to our hearts and our souls—
    We must guard them all if we want to be whole.

A soul that's at peace, a forgiving heart,
    Plus a mind that keeps growing would be a great
    start.
    Learning to flex—a key to the change gig—
    If we're rigid and harsh, the damage is big.

*Surprised by Old Age*

You know many old folks who are bitter and sour,
    While others are sweet until their last hour.
    Adapting to change takes courage and grit,
    'Cause old habits die hard—there's no doubting it.

No matter if we've "always done it this way,"
    Those five words can be toxic to say.
    When changes come, and surely they will,
    It's best to adjust and adapt with keen skill.

As I come near the end of the story I tell,
    All chapters point to finishing well.
    Regardless of rocks and bumps on the way,
    Being willing to change carries the day.

# A Reason To Live

*When Dr. Art Ammann experienced cardiac arrest, not once but three times at age 66, it was a life changing experience. He woke up in the ICU after the installation of a life-saving pacemaker and began a journey of questioning the gift of life in new ways. How would he live these extended moments, weeks or years differently? The following is excerpted from his Medtronics prize-winning essay that gives us unique insight into what it means to "finish well."*

In 1982, I did not realize the change that discovering and treating the first child with AIDS would bring. In the first decade, the intensity of the research, hundreds of speaking engagements, participation on advisory boards and travel throughout the U.S. to report the findings of the new epidemic left me exhausted. Thankfully, by the end we discovered all known means of transmission and several ways to treat the disease.

Then something unexpected happened. I had an emergency hospitalization for severe abdominal pain and during that time experienced cardiac arrest. I recovered from surgery and had a pacemaker installed to "keep me going."

After 10 days in the intensive care unit, as I recovered from the surgery at home, I reflected on the discoveries my collaborators and I had made throughout my career: formulating a vaccine which prevents pneumococcal infection and saved the lives of millions of children and elderly, and identifying the first child with AIDS and the first patient with blood transfusion AIDS. My career also included hundreds of publications, many awards, tenure as a full professor at the University of California, San Francisco Medical Center and a gratifying second career at Genentech, a highly successful biotechnology company. I was financially secure. Perhaps, I thought, it was time to retire.

One morning I read *The Imitation of Christ*, written in the 14th century by Thomas à Kempis. "God says to us, His children, it is necessary for you to learn many more things, which you have not yet learned well." I remember groaning out loud. Hadn't I learned enough? Hadn't I done enough? But then came more. "Various desires and aspirations often move you and drive you forward with enthusiasm; but you should consider whether you are motivated for my honor, or rather for your own success."

It was an unambiguous challenge. Justice was to be desired. I knew I had the resources to do something more. Medical advances had slowed the HIV epidemic in the U.S. but did not have a perceptible impact in developing countries where there were three to five million new infections each year, especially in women and children. I had been working with several foundations to address the HIV epidemic in the U.S., but I could not convince them that the problems in the resource-poor countries were of great urgency. My thoughts began to turn to starting a nonprofit foundation to concentrate on those issues.

It took several years to put together the framework of the foundation, define goals, as well as construct a Board of Advisors and a Board of Directors. In 1998, I founded Global Strategies for HIV Prevention.

Thanks to my stock holdings in Genentech, I did not need a salary or reimbursement for expenses. This meant we were able to operate entirely as a volunteer organization. Global Strategies continues to focus on life-threatening health care issues that confront women and children in some of the most neglected regions of the world. We've made great progress in identifying and providing treatment for HIV infection of women in politically unstable regions, that other organizations considered too difficult to tackle. We're also addressing infant mortality from other causes and bringing new technology into resource-poor areas. Together, we're providing a future of hope.

I now know why I survived cardiac arrest. It slowed me down just long enough to feel the weight of the need to address the issues of justice for those in desperate need in faraway places and to effect practical change.

We are under the illusion that rigidity and narrowing of life only begins in age, when actually they begin in the twenties and thirties or whenever we abandon the journey inward: and like any progressive disease, they become more evident with years.

—Elizabeth O'Connor [7]

---

7   Elizabeth O'Connor, *Journey Inward, Journey Outward*. (New York, HarperCollins, 1975).

# Slow Down and Let Go

Two of my lifetime heroes are Bill and Deanna Starr. Although Deanna is in her 70s, Bill has just turned 92. Deanna and I enjoyed catching up as we sipped iced tea on the patio of their hundred-year-old Idaho ranch house.

I placed my glass on the table and asked, "What has changed for you since our visit last year?"

Deanna replied in her gentle Idaho drawl, "Right now we are learning to slow down and let go."

Those words sent shivers up and down my spine. Even now, Jim and I live at an undeniably fast pace. We experience so many involvements with little or no space between travel, events and projects that require large amounts of preparation. Relationships rule our lives as we work at connecting with our large family and array of friends from decades past, such as the Starrs. Letting go and slowing down sounded like both heaven and hell to me.

In her lilting and peaceful way, Deanna spelled out the quiet rhythm of their ranch life in remote Rathdrum, Idaho. Bill's career in youth ministry through Young Life had taken him all around the world, speaking and teaching. His relentless schedule kept him away from his family much more than he would have liked. The pace of his life even affected him physically, as he suffered migraines during his busiest travel seasons.

Now, instead of traveling to others, Bill found that people from far and wide, like us, were coming to him. The change was obvious and attractive. I asked how it evolved. Deanna told me that Bill's physical health issues—from migraines to cancer and heart disease—had forced him to slow down and let go. Through all this, Deanna has modeled dedication and sacrificial love by her sweet and loyal care for Bill. Bill's depth of wisdom and experience fills the air with inspiration and challenge. In slowing down and letting go, they have visibly been filled and fill others with huge amounts of relational treasure—the most valuable being the gift of time, quiet, unrushed, no-agenda time. That's what I call a positive change.

My one lesson of the day: Go while you can. Let go when you must!

*Barbara McLennan*

# A Bucket of Change

*Georgia Ichen served as the head of the accounting department at Jim's company, McLennan Real Estate Company, for two decades. With her practical and quiet wisdom she mentored a number of younger people in the firm throughout that time. She and her husband have the gift of hospitality and have been dear friends through many of our changes.*

How did we get here in a world that has changed more during our years than in any other time in history? Well I know how I got here. It began with grandparents and in-laws who had the courage to come to America to begin a new life. While it was a blending of cultures from Wales, Italy and Poland, there was one constant. It was that these wonderful people shared a value system, which included a commitment to family and community. The basis for that commitment was faith. They taught us to value the principles and blessings of a loving God.

The question of how did "we" get here has puzzled me for quite some time. Indeed, our culture's bucket of change has overflowed with technology and the comforts of living. How have we adapted to the vast change? As a generation, we have adapted well to be able to use technology to enhance comfort, convenience, health, connectivity in a mobile society, and production of goods and services. There has been no problem in the willingness to see the need for and accepting the change.

The greater dilemma has been in how we have managed this change. Have we allowed our comfort to prevent us from properly managing these changes? Did we allow the media to promote lust as a way of life? Did we allow the enhanced production of food to promote gluttony to the point of an endemic problem with obesity? Did we allow the growth of credit to promote greed and the excessive pursuit of material possessions? Did we allow the daily conveniences of life and government programs to promote sloth and the stifling of development of our individual talents? Did we allow our freedom of speech to promote wrath in the form of uncontrollable hate and disrespect of others? Did we allow the position of others to promote envy and a lack of respect for those who strive to succeed? Did we allow positions of leadership to promote pride and lose sight of values of a good heart? Did we fail to manage change for the greater good of the community? Did we fail to keep God and Jesus Christ in the management of change?

As a generation, we lived in the best of times of America. In a discussion with our son some time ago, he affirmed that our generation and his have done a poor job of managing the changes. While it was nice of him to take a share of the responsibility, I do have to wonder if we, the older generation, finish well by leaving an America that is so divided, so confused about faith and has such a distorted value system? How can we hope to alter the management of change to move to reinforcing a new level of change that is more like the community that God and Jesus Christ prepared for us?

You may have heard the familiar story: A man walking along a beach sees hundreds of starfish that had been washed ashore in a storm. The man came upon a small boy who was picking up starfish and throwing them back in the sea. He said to the boy, "You cannot possibly hope to save all of those starfish." The little boy replied, "No, but I can make a difference for some." That rather sums up how I perceive finishing well in the face of the troubles in our culture.

I have learned that you cannot legislate what one holds in one's heart or the management of change. Rather, we must, first, believe in the power of prayer. Pray every day that people, including our leaders, will open their hearts to God and make decisions accordingly. Second, we must believe in and support a community of faith. Only faith can enlighten us and support us in times of challenge. Third, with gratitude great things happen: we must teach our family to "pay it forward" to the community. Perhaps the strength of one community at a time can make a difference. And so, I shall keep trying to finish well.

*The following two poems resulted from my collaboration with Norma Madsen, a dear forever friend. Norma provided the thoughts, which I turned into rhyme. She also contributed an essay to this book, which you can read in the next chapter.*

# Surprise!

I was so busy with the bucket I carried.
    Filled over full, I was tired and harried.
    Not truly feeling like a wise old sage,
    I found myself surprised by reaching old age.

There were just a few "elders" whom I enjoyed.
    Many I found that really annoyed—
    Like those in traffic or the grocery aisle,
    Bringing me nothing as nice as a smile.

In conversations they were disconnected—
    Found just a few whom I respected.
    Oh those old people, wouldn't you know it,
    Irked me so much I would nearly blow it.

They caused me to be sour and to be undone.
    I hate to admit it, but now I am one.

*Barbara McLennan*

# Truth In Old Age

Our Lord is patient, clever and wise
    In what He allows us to do.
    As we grow into our elder years,
    He shows us a path to what's true.

A pathway to truth feels downward it seems
    With uncomfortable stuff filled with pain.
    But that very truth can bring freedom to us
    Something we're eager to gain.

# Chapter Six

## The Honey Bucket[8]

Sadly, this bucket has come to mind—
    Not tidy or sweet, but the opposite kind.
    For you city slickers who've not heard that name
    A honey bucket and an outhouse are used much
    the same.

This bucket is smelly and yucky and foul.
    If buckets had faces, this one would sure scowl.
    Full of garbage, manure and other bad stuff
    We all have to deal with—things that are rough.

Any camper must know this part of camp life,
    Nasty but necessary, both day and night.

Sin is like that; it destroys and decays
    And must be handled—without delay,

---

8    Honey Bucket: A toilet that does not use water and must be emptied manually.

By repenting and confessing all that's within.
We obey God's decrees about what He calls sin.

On into aging, one thing is quite certain,
  This bucket must exit before "drawing the curtain."
  As ugly and painful as this process may be,
  Dumping this bucket makes one truly free.

Sin's price has been paid; I need bear it no more.
  Grace is the word that springs to the fore.
  God in His wisdom did what I couldn't do;
  He dumped my sin-bucket thus making me new.

*Barbara McLennan*

**It is easier to get older than it is to get wiser.**

—Anonymous

# Norma's Honey Bucket Story

*Norma Madsen is a forever friend. Though we shared some college years over half a century ago, now we're often apart for long periods of time. We always pick up at a deep level right where we left off. She is one who "tells it like it is" forthrightly, but gently. Norma has always had a gift for making me think. Since we seldom see each other, I find myself pondering her comments for weeks, even months afterward. Such was the case with this bucket.*

When we visited recently, I eagerly told Norma about my book idea, sensing she would contribute in some intriguing way. I was right! When I checked the mail a few days later, I found one of her lengthy letters, handwritten as always on yellow legal paper. I quickly incorporated both of her "bucket ideas" into the mix. She pointed out that Jesus himself literally had no bucket when he met that Samaritan woman at the well. It was such a true "Norma thing" to think of. I loved it and immediately went to work to capture her insight, chiding myself that I hadn't already thought of that. (See the results of our conversation in Chapter 9.)

The other suggestion was a bit of a conundrum to me. The "Honey Bucket" jokingly came up during our visit. After we had a good laugh about the rawness of it, Norma's assessment turned serious. "We really must get rid of the garbage in our lives to enjoy old age. We drag around bags of nasty stuff; we put off dealing with unhealthy, downright destructive issues until we can no longer stand it. Sometimes too late."

Hmmm, something to think about. But would I have the nerve to include a chapter titled "The Honey Bucket"? I realized that some city people have never even heard of a honey bucket. Would it be terribly offensive to them? What does that have to do with old age and surprises anyway? More questions than answers. My introductory poem to the chapter came easily, but my questions lingered.

Many people say that, as we age, we lose our filter and tend to just say what we think. If our thinking has been polluted by sin, pain, and other unresolved issues, that's what will come out of our mouths and hearts. As difficult as it is to deal with sin, I'm realizing it is essential.

"Some men grow old gracefully. Age softens their faces, they get sweeter as the days go by, while others get sour and unsociable. It is important to know why we get one way or the other because all of us are getting older every day," writes David Roper. "Old age can be 'good old age' or it can be very bad; it depends on the route we take."[9]

Part of that route has to do with how we deal with sin in our lives. Keeping anger and bitterness inside will not make us "sweeter as the days go by."

---

9  David Roper, *The Strength of A Man* (Grand Rapids, Discovery House Publishers, 1989)

Still, to think of emptying a honey bucket is indelicate. Even the name is sarcastic and ironic. Honey? Seriously? In a recent letter, Norma zoned in with some brutal reminders of the reality of this bucket, like it or not. She emphasized the daily-ness of this chore. Even our bodies uphold this rule of nature, calling attention to our own systems when they get stopped up or blocked somehow.

"In fact," said Norma, "Jesus compared the community of believers to the body of Christ, urging us to take good care." Then, of all things, she quoted the Lord's Prayer, which teaches us to ask for forgiveness of our sins as we forgive those who sin against us, and added her commentary on this delicate subject. "It is our daily need to be relieved of sins and resentments that block the emptying of life's undigested stuff every day. Forgiving myself and others is an old and not-so-simple remedy for grumpiness and bitterness in old age. So the honey bucket reminds us to deal with stinkin' relationships before 'the end.'" She concluded by writing this: "You and I both know the promise of dealing with the not-so-nice parts of ourselves. This brings the freedom to live and die a joyful old age, full of Holy Spirit gratitude and grace."

It is clear to me once again why Norma is a forever friend.

*Barbara McLennan*

**We are too soon old and too late smart.**

—Dutch Proverb

*The following poem was created using thoughts and ideas from Bruce Watson, an old friend from Vancouver B.C.*

# Forgiveness

The honey bucket mocks us by its very name;
> nothing sweet about this thing, yet there it is, in
> reality.

The garbage we carry in our hearts and minds can be
> just as toxic and nasty
> as any bucket you might imagine.

Holding on to hurtful, harmful stuff from the past
> leaves stench and stain,
> in time causing us to hide or withdraw.

Letting go of that bucket is not easy, but holding on to it
> is harder.

Dragging behind us a heavy bag of shadows, mixed in
> with the un-forgiveness
> of old garbage is no way to live life—and a worse
> way to end life.

Hard feelings grow bitter roots, deep and twisted,
> strangling quality of life,
> robbing a person of all joy and freedom, holding
> victims captive
> until all memory of the original wrong evaporates.

Forgiveness is like oil to loosen the grip; an elixir of
   healing
   and freedom from guilt and shame for both parties.

Those who forgive are first to be freed, even as bondage
   lifts from the other.

Pain is the enemy—forgiveness, the olive branch.

Jesus once told a group of indignant, angry men to drop
   their stones and rocks
   as He told a trembling woman "go and sin no
   more."

Every time you make a choice, you are turning the
central part of you, the part of you that chooses,
into something a little different from what it was
before. And taking your life as a whole, with all
your innumerable choices, all your life long, you are
slowly turning this central thing either into a heavenly
creature or into a hellish creature: either into a creature
that is in harmony with God, and with other creatures
and with itself, or else into one that is in a state of war
and hatred with God, and with its fellow-creatures, and
with itself. To be the one kind of creature is heaven:
that is, it is joy and peace and knowledge and power.
To be the other means madness, horror, idiocy, rage,
impotence, and eternal loneliness. Each of us at each
moment is progressing to one state or the other. [10]

—C.S. Lewis

10   C.S. Lewis, *Mere Christianity* (San Francisco, HarperOne, 2001),
      86-87.

# Chapter Seven

## Shootin' Buckets

This game needs a ball and a bucket, or hoop—
    Stuck to a post to gather a group.
    A player must shoot the ball over the rim,
    Racking up points, so their team can win.

Big boys or little, grandpas or dads—
    Even girls and moms love to play with the lads.
    Never too young, never too old—
    A game for all ages, so I am told.

The point of all this is simply to "play,"
    Finding some game to break up each day.

Old folks need play too; it's a sure bet!
    We turn sour and cranky if by chance we forget.
    At any age, play feeds body and spirit—
    For both kinds of "heart," it's crucial to hear it.

So just wad up some paper and shoot for a rim
    Of a scrub bucket or waste bin, and try for a win.
    Keep inventing amusing new ways to play,
    Laugh and relax and have fun every day.

No matter the score, you'll be wanting more fun,
    And you'll find old age blues will soon come
    undone.

# The Family that Plays Together

Second only to our strong Christian faith, play has been a sure foundation and bonding factor in our 60-plus years of family history. I believe playing has helped us navigate our senior years with a bit more energy and a sense of humor. And it definitely drew our family together.

Even back in our courting years, we used sports and games to build our friendship as a couple. Every weekend, we tossed the canoe onto the car top for local adventures, including more than one "accidental" tipping into bracing cold lake water, evoking peals of laughter. We'd find any excuse to visit friends or relatives owning powerboats, which just happened to provide us with opportunities to waterski and swim. Basketball and softball leagues filled our weekly schedule with recreation and social connections. Even on a quiet day, we would pull out Monopoly or Dominoes, pop a big batch of popcorn, and have game night with friends. These interactions set the playful tone for our relationship—and soon after college, our marriage.

Our first child, Tami Joy, never knew life without wearing her bulky, yellow life jacket and being held tightly in someone's lap while endless water-skiing turns took place.

As our family grew, so did play. Snow skiing adventures began early (as soon as diapers were a thing of the past). Our four kids graduated from local bunny ski hills to the grand Colorado Rockies. Trips always included extra folks—such as a grandmother to babysit the very youngest. Often, certain cousins, or whole families with kids near the same ages as ours, joined us, bonding and building memorable experiences, learning skills and passion for sports and friendships that would last a lifetime.

Jim's foresighted parents invested in a summer lake property when we'd been married about four years. Wisely, they chose a place within an hour's drive from our home, making it easily available in all seasons. This would become the epicenter of play, not only for our family of six but also for an extended family of aunts, uncles and cousins, which now, over a half century later, still gather there. On holidays, about 35 of us crowd into the house. On ordinary weekends, there are often more people than beds, but we always make do.

Our family traditions at the lake include hilarious skits, trampoline competitions, kayak races, and waterskiing for all ages (including me until my 73rd birthday). Our youngest skier ever was three-year-old Davis, who recently skied by himself on the boat boom with Uncle Todd's coaching. The teenagers and their buddies were delighted with the recent addition of a pickle ball court as well as sand volleyball.

Winters didn't keep us inside; everyone loved sledding and tobogganing, broom hockey and ice-skating. As the short winter days grew dark, we'd build a bonfire on the beach, enjoy hot chocolate and s'mores, and share scary ghost stories and spontaneous campfire songfests.

Whether the senior generation is watching from the warmth of the house or the next younger generation is playing on the beach, I feel tremendous satisfaction in witnessing the family ties and bonding of this place over the many years.

The lake house offers us a continuous excuse to play. It helped us uphold our lifelong exercise mantra as we grow older, "Move it or lose it."

In addition, one of the most important by-products of play by far is that it provides opportunity to hone the art of grandparenting. Our eldest grandchild, Ellen, is now 31; our youngest, Brantley, is 7. The very youngest great-grand, Molly, is presently four months old. Over the years I have narrowed down my grandparent role to two major categories. The first is to simply love them. Finding ways to do this is not difficult, yet includes tough love, unconditional (as possible) love, and plying them with treats until they behave (if necessary). It turns out that loving your grandchildren is a prime way to show love to your own children and their spouses.

My second role is that of a story-teller. It can start with bedtime read-aloud books, which involves lots of snuggling. But it also includes such categories as real life stories, make believe escapades, tales of their mom or dad when they were young, facts of family history, and stories of the faith. A very important ingredient is to include each child in each and every story.

To add a dimension to a well-worn saying, "The family that prays together *and plays* together stays together."

Fun is important at every age but can be even more beneficial as we grow older. The very things associated with it—laughter, levity, enjoyment, diversion—can act as antidotes to stress, depression, and anxiety. It often involves being with others, and social connections are linked to better cognitive health in later life and lower likelihood of developing dementia.[11]

—Clare Ansberry

11  From Clare Ansberry, "An Overlooked Skill in Aging: How to Have Fun," The Wall Street Journal, June 2, 2018. https://www.wsj.com/articles/an-overlooked-skill-in-aging-how-to-have-fun-1527937260

# Chapter Eight

## No Bucket[12]

They met at midday at Jacob's well—
    A multi-layered story their meeting does tell.
    She was trapped in tradition, under laws of old—
    An historic conversation began to unfold.

He was thirsty and tired and asked for a drink—
    Not too unreasonable, a person might think.
    But a Samaritan woman? And a man who's a Jew?
    Her forefathers ruled that was truly taboo.

"If you knew who I am and what I can do,
    Living Water'd flow freely," he said, "just for you."
    "But you have no bucket, and this well is deep—
    Where our Father Jacob watered his sheep."

---

12 Inspired by John 4:1-30.

"Drink of that water, and your thirst will return—
   Mine is eternal, for which all hearts do yearn."
   He went on to reveal for the very first time"
   I am Messiah—God's promise Divine."

Because of this woman, many townsmen believed
   He is the Savior to all who receive.

No telling what happens when we join this story
   Of His Living Water, which brings us to Glory.
   So many lessons from this tale of old—
   I find new insights each time it is told.

An "invisible" woman, despised by most,
   Discovered Messiah, her Jacob's Well host.
   He did not guilt her, nor riddle her with shame,
   Instead He gave value by revealing His name.

"Messiah I am, and I care about you—
   Go bring the others so they can hear too.
   My fresh, living water is open to all,
   I'll fill your bucket when you answer my call."

*Barbara McLennan*

# The Inner Well of Gratitude

*My friend Norma Madsen wrote the following reflection about the story of Jesus' encounter with the Samaritan woman at the well from John 4.*

For me, the blessing of old age is seeing and hearing Jesus in a new way—His friendly smile as He offers to take my heavy bucket and gives me His arm instead. He offers to walk with me as slowly as need be until I am free enough to dance again, or simply free enough to sit and enjoy watching the dance with others younger than I am. I turn the old bucket upside down and sit on it as I witness what the risen Christ, God's Holy Spirit, is doing in and through others. Some know they are God's children, and some don't, but they are doing God's work proclaiming good news for the poor, the release for the captives and care for victims, just like the Good Samaritan who helped and provided for a stranger as though he had been neighbor and friend to the injured one.

All of this primes an inner well of gratitude—filling me with thanksgiving and praise. I am so grateful to see others (as well as myself) with new, restored eyes, so I can know we are part of God's new creation—an artesian well of living water, no bucket needed!

Old age can be a time to discover the intimacy with God Jesus promised us.

**This is how to grow old.**

**Allow everything else to fall away
until those around you see only love.**[13]

—John Ortberg

---

13 John Ortberg, *The Me I Want to Be* (Grand Rapids, Zondervan, 2010).

# Another Well, Another Woman

*Ruth Madsen (no relation to Norma) is a gifted story-teller,*
*an inspiration to me and another forever friend. She wrote the*
*following essay, where she takes us to another well, where as a*
*very young girl, she too, encounters Jesus.*

I had a million-dollar childhood, especially during
summer months! Our family was one of many on
Norwegian Hill near Lake Geneva, Wisconsin. The
families were all Norwegian, all friends of ours and all
from Salem Norwegian Church of Chicago. One weekend
the men had come together, driving in tandem, to search
out a vacation spot of clean air and woods for their wives
and children. They desired to move far from the noise,
dirt and heat of Chicago.

They settled in the beautiful, wooded hills of the kindest
farmer in Wisconsin, Mr. Southwick, who welcomed
us with genuine love. We returned summer after
summer. Alongside Mr. Southwick, we all attended his
little church, Calvary. He parceled off a vast acreage of
rolling landscape and wooded hills for purchase by the
families, allowing them to progress over the years from
their initial tents, to tents on platforms, to little cottages
without electricity or water and beyond.

We thought it was sheer luxury. Summers as children
were glorious days filled with climbing hills and ravines,
helping Mr. Southwick milk the cows, and riding on the
top of his hay wagon as it made its dubious way over

the rough path winding back down to the barn. We went berry picking in the ravines, spent exhilarating hours on the beach of Williams Bay, and delighted in mid-week picnics and smorgasbords on Saturday around a blazing fire. Kerosene lamps took care of the lack of electricity, but we had to solve the water need. We collected and saved rainwater for our little flower gardens. Drinking water came from a flowing creek near Mr. Southwick's home, which was quite some distance from our cottage.

It became my assignment to keep our own family's drinking water supply filled. This involved grabbing my bucket, trekking down the wooded hill, opening the huge gate at the bottom, passing into the farmer's pasture avoiding snakes and cows, arriving at the fresh water creek where a well was constructed. This was the source of my water. However, I was a young girl, and the bucket was heavier than I could manage. I struggled to carry a full bucket over uneven and rocky terrain, the handle digging into my palms and fingers. I strained back up the hill to the cottage with the water sloshing and splashing along the way as I half tripped and recovered this way and that. By the time my journey ended, my bucket would be only partially full, much of the water having spilled out with each step on the trek home.

I complained to my parents, suggesting that the task was more appropriate for a stronger person. My father looked at me kindly but said nothing. A day later he presented me with a yoke he constructed from a piece of wood— just for me. Each end now held a bucket. He walked with me to the creek that day, loaded the buckets with water and showed me how I could now carry two buckets, with twice the weight as before, as long as I used the yoke. He was right. It worked! Not only did I handle double the load, but I also had little spillage because I completely relied on the yoke my father had fashioned just for me.

Years later, as I remember this experience, a lesson surfaces. As we approach old age and are surprised by the unexpected burdens that come our way, it is clear that our heavenly Father never intended that we bear that load alone. He fashioned a yoke, just as my earthly father did for me. No longer do we need to fear the heavy bucket that comes with age—a bucket often filled with loneliness, fears, loss of abilities, pain, strapped finances, separations, unknowns, death—weight we cannot bear alone. Instead, we need to hook our buckets to the yoke. Jesus said it this way:

*"Take my yoke upon you and learn from me, for I am gentle and humble in heart, and you will find rest for your souls. For my yoke is easy and my burden is light."*

Matthew 11:28 - 30

# Chapter Nine

## Kicking the Bucket—Finishing Well

"Kick the bucket"—an idiom that's crass.
  But it's just a name for the time when we pass.
  It's merely a marker at the end of our road,
  An honest reality we hate to behold.

Those who have lived well, finish well too,
  With peace and contentment, when life here is
  through.
  How then to prepare to face our conclusion
  Kicking out fear or even confusion?

God knows all of our days before we live even one
  Giving freedom and peace when our time here is
  done.
  He knows all about us, both outside and in—
  So He sent His one Son to forgive all our sin.

He guides and directs with His loving hand,
 No matter our place—on sea or on land.
 Perhaps we're surprised as we enter old age,
 But He's got us covered as we come to this stage.

Our only part—to believe, trust and love—
 He fills us with grace, which comes from above.
 All chapters point to finishing well,
 As I've listened to those whose stories I tell.

Regardless of rocks and bumps on the way,
 It's faith in Jesus that carries the day.
 No matter what trial, sin, guilt or shame,
 God's love, grace and mercy are stamped on
 each name.

He knows us and welcomes us home when it's time.
 Are we ready and eager for the grand "finish line"?

# Psalm 139:1-6; 16

Lord, you have searched me and you know me.

You know when I stand and when I rise,

You perceive my thoughts from afar.

You discern my going out and my lying down;

you are familiar with all my ways.

Before a word is on my tongue you know it completely,
O Lord.

You hem me in behind and before;

you have laid your hand upon me.

Such knowledge is too wonderful for me,

Too lofty for me to attain.


All the days ordained for me

Were written in your book

Before one of them came to be.

# A Legacy of Character

Character, it's said, is about who you are when no one is looking. Events and actions unintended for public awareness may become part of a precious and valued legacy. Such was the case with William C. McLennan, Jim's paternal grandfather.

Having emigrated from Scotland in the early 1900s, the son of a poor mining family, he traveled from Pennsylvania to Illinois to Colorado to Alaska to Washington and finally settled in as a bricklayer in Chicago. In 1912, he proudly founded a homebuilding and real estate company on the northwest edge of Chicago.

In the teens and twenties, he built over five thousand homes. He served both as builder and lender, as he made a practice of taking the mortgages for many homebuyers. He would then consolidate the mortgages and sell them to a prosperous Chicago bank. Suddenly came the 1929 stock market crash and the Great Depression. What was unknown to his family and business partners (his three grown sons) became a true legacy at his death in his 86th year…in fact, on the first day of his wake.

The story unfolded as Jim, William's grandson, was appointed to represent the family in the early afternoon hours of the wake. Young Jim was chosen because very few people were expected to arrive in the first hours of the several day wake. His dad and two uncles were scheduled to take over after the dinner hour and throughout the rest of the evening. When Jim arrived, much to his surprise, he saw a line out the front door of the funeral home and down the sidewalk and the rest of the city block. Jim hustled to take his place near the casket and began greeting people.

One after another those coming to pay their respects with gratitude and honor told similar stories. Jim heard of how Grandpa McLennan had intervened when the big city bank ruthlessly called in the mortgages and demanded payments, even when the loans were only thirty days past due. Early in the game of foreclosure William heard of this injustice. He marched into the bank president's office and promptly bought back all the mortgages he had previously sold to them. He then went back to the homeowners and dealt with them individually, with kindness and mercy, allowing them to stay in their homes, receiving any payment they could afford at a given time.

One after another Jim heard from these grateful folks:

"We could never have stayed in our home without Mr. McLennan's help." "We would have been out in the street if weren't for him."

"We will never forget his kindness."

"He kept our financial future intact."

After a short while, Jim realized his father and uncles should be experiencing this outpouring of testimony about their father. They immediately responded to his call and intercepted this parade of grateful families as it continued for the rest of the wake.

This kind and humble man of high principles had never revealed his act of mercy and kindness to his business partners. As word reached the rest of his relatives, the story became etched in family history. To him, it was simply the right and ethical thing to do. This ongoing act of grace and compassion remains a powerful example that we pass down from one generation to the next. We shared it again recently at a family reunion where more than one hundred of the "kith and kin" gathered—all cousins directly related to William C. McLennan, the patriarch of the clan.

His legacy lives on as a model for the business he founded in 1912, well over a hundred years ago, which is still going strong in the fourth generation of family ownership.

In addition to his legacy of kindness and wisdom in business, William also bequeathed his family with a spiritual legacy. Every single morning, he and his wife Jessie prayed for their six children and 19 grandchildren, by name, as well as for the family's generations yet unborn. At that family reunion, some 90 percent of the cousins were still walking in the faith—a tribute to William and Jessie's faithful prayers.

What a prime example of finishing well!

# Specific Intentions for Finishing Well

*In the final pages of a book titled* Musings, *written by our lifelong friend, Kent Hotaling, he offers some thought-provoking questions and insights about how we approach old age. As far back as the 1960s, Kent and his wife, Kay, had a unique way of cultivating deep relationships with a few, deeply sharing life and times. A handful of such friends met with him and affirmed these thoughts on specific aspects of their lives to equip them to finish well as they entered their sixties and seventies.*

Time:  It is essential that we come to agreement about a joint vision with our spouses as to how we are to use our time, energy and money.

Calling:  Understanding the present calling of God on our lives is essential. Is it the same one with which we began? How has it changed over time? What is it to be in this latter phase of our lives?

Health:  We have no control over many health issues that come in later life, but we can be diligent in exercise, food discipline, and living with less stress—we have some control over these.

People:  One factor in the opportunities we have to serve the Lord in the latter phase is to discover who wants to be with us. Have we lived in such a way that people are seeking time with us?

Discernment: It is very desirable to have close companions who can walk with us to help us discern and deal with the important issues in our lives.

Pace: We want to learn to live at a slower pace as energy lessens but at the same time refuse to plateau or to tread water spiritually.

**Even when I am old and gray, do not forsake me O God, 'til I declare your power to the next generation, your might to all who are to come.**

Psalm 71:18

Barbara McLennan

# "I Wish Everyone Could Feel This Peace"

*In the two weeks before he died, Skip Sippert's family wrote down some of the things he told them. We heard his story from Doug Barram, a longtime friend of ours who knew Skip and his family well. Skip's family created this list based on their conversations with him, and on how he lived his final days. He was truly a man who finished well. I hope and pray that I, and my loved ones, will end our lives with the kind of peace and joy that Skip not only experienced but also gave to others, even in his final days.*

These are the best two weeks of my whole life.

Nothing else matters; I just want to see Jesus' face.

I was awake last night and saw two figures in bright white standing over me on each side of the bed. I wasn't afraid. They made me feel calm.

I can't describe how peaceful I feel. I wish everyone could feel this peace. It's so wonderful I can't explain it.

God is merciful. I don't have any pain.

All my life my prayers have been scattered; easy to lose focus. Now they have such clarity, unwavering focus and connection.

There is nothing to pray about for myself. God knows everything about me. I lie here and just want to pray for everyone else.

I feel so blessed to have had 75 years to enjoy.

With each and every one of your calls or visits or cards that were read aloud to me, I closed my eyes tightly and remembered aloud how precious you are and your families are to me, and I thanked God for the privilege of knowing you.

How comforting it was to be in my own bed, wrapped in my quilts the ladies [from church] made. How I loved those quilts. (Skip had been asked to deliver the quilts these ladies made to Helpline and each time he would say "I really like this one. Can I have it?" He has three or four of them.)

Most of all, I wished over and over again that every one of you could feel this immense peace that I am bathed in. I didn't want to let go because I was enjoying this peace and joy so much.

In the three days before his death, Skip told his family that each time he opened his eyes, the room was filled with a bright, white light that reached down to him. They were reminded that Jesus said, "I am the light." In the end, our relationship with Jesus is what matters.

His family shared these precious memories to encourage others to finish well. Death is inevitable, but finishing well takes intention. The best way to finish well, if Skip is any example, is to focus on Jesus throughout your life.

# Time to Fly

*Char was one of my life-long heroes. She was an accomplished writer dedicated to Jesus and one of the prominent early leaders of Young Life youth ministry. This snippet was taken from a letter written to her son in 1993. She went to be with Jesus in 2016. Her dear, dear friend and mine was Bill Starr (now age 93). When he read this, he laughed a hearty laugh and proclaimed, "You go girl; that's the way to tell it." They both top my list for finishing well.*

"When my time to fly out of this old human frame apparently arrives, I am ready to go!

"Stand back, my son, and watch me FLY!

"Don't get in my way, please. God has given me an exciting and marvelous life…

"I love life, and I love you…but I do believe with all my heart, with Paul, that 'to be present with the Lord is far better.'"

**⁶ So we are always confident, knowing that while we are at home in the body we are absent from the Lord. ⁷ For we walk by faith, not by sight. ⁸ We are confident, yes, well pleased rather to be absent from the body and to be present with the Lord.**

2 Corinthians 5:6-8, NKJV

**As my Grandma used to say:**
**Until further notice...**

**CELEBRATE EVERYTHING!** [14]

---

14   From a speech by Brennan Manning